The Lost Railways of Northumbe...
by Bernard Byrom

LAMBLEY VIADUCT.

Acknowledgements

The publisher wishes to thank the following for contributing photographs to this book: John Alsop for the back cover and pages 1, 4, 5, 7, 8, 9, 11, 12, 13, 14, 15, 17, 18, 20, 21, 22, 23, 24, 25, 27, 28, 29, 32, 33, 34, 37, 44, 45, 46, 48 (both); and Richard Casserley for pages 16, 35, 40, 43

Ponteland Station.

Kirknewton Station.

Introduction

The railways of Northumberland were made up of two extremes. On the one hand there was industrial North Tyneside with an intensive passenger and freight service which accounted for the bulk of the region's income and also the express passenger route up what is now the East Coast Main Line between Newcastle and Berwick. On the other hand, there were several unrenumerative rural lines, some of which were built in anticipation of traffic that never materialised and some that were built by one railway company as 'blocking' lines to thwart a rival company's incursions into what the first company regarded as its own rightful territory and which it went to great (and often expensive) lengths to defend against all competition.

At the time these lines were built the principal railway company in Northumberland was the North Eastern Railway. This railway had a virtual monopoly of railways to the south in County Durham and a good part of North Yorkshire so, as far as Northumberland was concerned, it wasn't worried about competition coming from the south. However, it was a different matter to the north and northwest where the North British Railway, a great but often impecunious railway, was desperate to gain access to the riches of the Newcastle area.

All that are left today of railways in this vast county are the East Coast Main Line between Newcastle and Berwick, the cross-country line linking Newcastle and Carlisle and the parts of the Tyneside network that have been converted into the Tyneside Metro. This book attempts to show the passenger-carrying lines that have been lost forever; some were quite short branch lines but others wended their way for miles across desolate moorland. It is questionable whether these lines were ever viable, even as feeders to the main line, but the advent of the internal combustion engine and electric propulsion around the beginning of the twentieth century meant that buses and trams eventually became the public's preferred means of transport; the affordability of private motor cars in the 1950s sealed the branch lines' fate. Although Dr Beeching is generally blamed for decimating the railway network, it will be seen from the closure dates in this book that many of the Northumbrian rural lines had already been closed before his work began.

3

Allendale Branch

Passenger service withdrawn	22 September 1930	*Stations closed*	*Date of closure*
Distance	12 ¼ miles	Langley	22 September 1930
Company	Hexham & Allendale Railway	Staward	22 September 1930
		Allendale *	22 September 1930

Stations closed	*Date of closure*
Elrington	22 September 1930

* Originally named Catton Road until 1 May 1898.

Langley Station, *c*.1904.

This line was primarily constructed to transport lead ore from the mines in upland Northumberland to Hexham and onward to Newcastle-upon-Tyne. There were extensive lead mines at Allenheads and in the nineteenth century the small town of Allendale, 800 feet above sea level and seven miles north of Allenheads, expanded to become a very prosperous lead mining centre.

On 29 November 1864 a Bill was submitted to Parliament by the Hexham & Allendale Railway Company and this received the Royal Assent on 19 June the following year. It proposed to build a 13 ½ -mile single-track branch from Border Counties Junction at Hexham on the Newcastle & Carlisle Railway to Allendale with intermediate stations at Elrington, Langley and Staward but allowed the section from Allendale town to Allenheads to be omitted if financial or other problems were encountered. The North Eastern Railway was so enthusiastic about the line's potential that it subscribed £10,000 towards its initial cost.

Allendale Station, *c.*1909.

The line opened for freight as far as Langley on 19 August 1867, to Catton Road on 13 January 1868 and, following a delay owing to lack of funds to complete passenger facilities, the passenger service to Allendale commenced on 1 March 1869. From the outset the line was operated by the North Eastern Railway who took over full ownership on 13 July 1876. The engines used on the branch were F8 2-4-2T and G5 0-4-4T classes which were shedded at Hexham. Unfortunately for the line's prosperity, as early as 1870 the lead industry in the area started to decline and because of this the Allendale town extension and the further seven-mile extension to Allenheads were not built. In 1898 the North Eastern Railway surveyed but abandoned an extension into Allendale town and simply renamed Catton Road as Allendale. By the 1920s the industry had totally collapsed and so it was no surprise when the line was closed to passenger traffic on 22 September 1930, a casualty of the Great Depression. Goods traffic lingered on for another twenty years until the line was finally closed to all traffic on 20 November 1950.

The branch left the Newcastle & Carlisle Railway just west of Hexham at the Border Counties Junction and immediately curved southwest to climb into the hills, mainly on gradients of 1 in 50 and 1 in 60 to beyond Elrington. From there the line continued curving southwest and climbed to the summit of the line beyond Langley before dropping down into Allendale. Beyond this station was a 42-foot turntable with coal cells on the east and a loop line for the locomotive to run round its train. The station was situated about a mile from the town centre and was laid out as a through station for the intended line onwards to Allenheads. The station house is now the headquarters and office of the Allendale Caravan Park whilst the ground floor waiting rooms and ticket office are now a self-catering holiday flat. Both platforms at Langley survive; the former station is now privately owned and has been turned into a large garden that has become a minor tourist attraction.

The passenger service changed very little during the branch's lifetime – 33 minutes for the Hexham to Allendale journey and 30 minutes for the return. In 1920 there were three trains in each direction on weekdays plus an extra afternoon train to Hexham and back on Tuesday for Hexham market day. The Sunday service was one train in either direction.

Alnwick Branch

Passenger service withdrawn	29 January 1968
Distance	3 miles
Company	Newcastle & Berwick Railway

Stations closed	*Date of closure*
Alnwick (first station)	5 September 1887
Alnwick (second station)	29 January 1968

The Newcastle & Berwick Railway Act of 31 July 1845 empowered that railway to build a double-track branch line from its main line at Bilton Junction to the town of Alnwick three miles away. Following completion of its line between Gateshead and Berwick in 1848, construction of the branch began and it opened for goods on 5 August 1850 and for passengers a fortnight later. Leaving the East Coast Main Line at Bilton Junction (which was renamed Alnmouth in May 1892) it climbed on a gradient of 1 in 176, which steepened to 1 in 77, up to the town of Alnwick.

The original Alnwick Station was situated on the edge of town at the end of a waggonway from the Shilbottle Colliery. It had a single platform with a stone single-storey building containing offices and waiting rooms, a large stone goods warehouse and a signal box at the south end of the station yard. In 1885, when the additional branch from Alnwick to Cornhill was under construction, Alnwick Council asked the North Eastern Railway for improved facilities at the station and, to cope with the anticipated increase in traffic, a brand new terminal station with a wide island platform was built and opened on 5 September 1887. A new signal box was also built on the rail approach to the station and sometime around 1898 a wooden refreshment room was built on the platform. The old station site is nowadays a tyre depot.

At first the line was very busy; by the end of the century there were 60 trains a day using Alnwick Station and in 1911 there were 45 passenger trains a day between Alnmouth and Alnwick. But by the 1920s road transport was taking business away. By 1923 the number of weekday trains between Alnmouth and Alnwick had been reduced to sixteen, six of them being through services from Newcastle and three from Berwick with the latter needing to reverse at Alnmouth. The remainder were purely local trains between Alnwick and Alnmouth. In the opposite direction there were 15 trains of which six were for Newcastle, one for Berwick and one for Kelso. There were eight local trains in each direction on Sundays.

A Royal occasion at Alnwick Station.

After 1957, when the last NER 4-4-0s had been scrapped, the services were worked by various classes of locomotive, notably V1 and V3 2-6-2Ts and K1 2-6-0s. In 1964 the line was reduced to single track and the signalling removed. The last day of steam operation was 18 June 1966 with Class 9F 2-10-0 No. 92099 brought in specially to honour the occasion. Alnmouth's small two-road engine shed closed the same day and the branch began to be worked by DMUs. However, not even they could stem the tide – the passenger service was reduced still further and was finally withdrawn on 29 January 1968, the goods services carrying on until 7 November. After the closure the signal boxes, coal depot and weigh cabins were demolished but some buildings, including the goods shed, were rebuilt at Beamish in 1975. The 1887 station building is still in very good condition and in use as a carpet warehouse and a second-hand book emporium called Barter Books. In 1995 the Aln Valley Railway Society was formed with the aim of rebuilding the line and reopening it as a tourist attraction.

Alnwick — Cornhill

Passenger service withdrawn	22 September 1930
Distance	35 1/2 miles
Company	North Eastern Railway

Stations closed	*Date of closure*
Edlingham	22 September 1930
Whittingham	22 September 1930
Glanton	22 September 1930
Hedgeley	22 September 1930
Wooperton	22 September 1930

Stations closed	*Date of closure*
Ilderton	22 September 1930
Wooler	22 September 1930
Akeld	22 September 1930
Kirknewton	22 September 1930
Mindrum	22 September 1930
Coldstream *	15 June 1964 (see Tweedmouth to Kelso Branch)

* Originally named Cornhill until 1 October 1873.

Whittingham Station, *c.*1914.

In 1881 the Central Northumberland Railway proposed building a line from Rothbury to Wooler to open up rural Northumberland. This line had the backing of the North British Railway who already had a line southwards from Rothbury and were the North Eastern Railway's commercial rivals in the area. To counter this threat, and after pressure from local traders, landowners and politicians who didn't want to see agricultural traffic from the Wooler area diverted to Rothbury, the North Eastern proposed a branch line of its own from its station at Alnwick to the border town of Cornhill-on-Tweed where it would make a junction with its existing line from Tweedmouth to Kelso. Both proposals went before Parliament in 1881 and the North Eastern's Cornhill line was chosen because it was by far the cheaper, its construction cost being estimated at exactly £272,266.15.3d.

By virtue of the Alnwick & Cornhill Railway Act, passed on 19 May 1882, the North Eastern Railway began building a single track line of 35½ miles from the Alnwick end on 12 January 1884, opening it to goods between Cornhill and Wooperton on 2 May 1887. The company opened it throughout to passenger and goods services on 5 September from the new enlarged station at Alnwick and graced it with some of the finest station buildings ever provided on a rural branch line. The reason they did this remains a mystery; the line passed through sparsely populated country where four of the villages after which the stations were named had a population of less than 100 and most of the stations were a long way from the communities they served.

Leaving Alnwick, the line firstly swung south and climbed on a gradient of 1 in 50 with sharp curves for four miles over difficult terrain in order to avoid the Duke of Northumberland's estate before turning west and descending at 1 in 50 for two miles to Edlingham. There were frequent changes of gradient on the route and it was necessary to construct both a viaduct and tunnel between Edlingham and Whittingham. This is a great sheep breeding and rearing area and the sales required numerous specials to distribute the sheep to their new owners. On the other hand, passenger traffic was always light and even in 1911 there were only three passenger trains a day in each direction worked by Alnmouth and Tweedmouth engines, some of which ran via the main line in one direction and via Coldstream and Wooler in the other. In 1923 there were still three trains from Alnwick to Coldstream, two of them working through to Tweedmouth whilst in the opposite direction one train originated at Tweedmouth and another at Berwick. The usual locomotives in the 1920s were classes D20 4-4-0s from Tweedmouth Shed and D17/1 4-4-0s from Alnmouth, amongst them the famous No. 1621 that had distinguished itself running between Newcastle and Edinburgh in the 1895 Races to the North.

Akeld Station, 14 April 1963.

Traffic on the line never approached its promoters' expectations and the branch became another casualty of the Great Depression, closing to passenger traffic on 22 September 1930. Even though passenger services had ceased, the London & North Eastern Railway still provided camping coaches at a number of stations on the line, to which holidaymakers were taken in carriages attached to the daily parcels trains. Many station buildings and platforms were left in situ after the passenger service was withdrawn and these have since been converted into handsome private houses. The goods service continued using the line until 12 August 1948 when floods washed out a bridge south of Mindrum, causing the line to be operated in two sections, Alnwick to Kirknewton and Coldstream to Mindrum. When further floods on 26 October 1949 washed out another bridge between Wooler and Ilderton, a decision was taken to repair the Mindrum bridge and to operate the line in two sections, this time Alnwick to Ilderton and Coldstream to Wooler. On 2 March 1953 the Alnwick to Ilderton section was closed and the track lifted, followed by the Coldstream to Wooler section on 29 March 1965.

Alnwick — Cornhill

Alston Branch *

Passenger service withdrawn	3 May 1976	*Stations closed*	*Date of closure*
Distance	13 miles	Lambley	3 May 1976
Company	Newcastle & Carlisle Railway	Slaggyford	3 May 1976

Stations closed	*Date of closure*
Penmeller Halt	1932
Featherstone Park **	3 May 1976
Coanwood ***	3 May 1976

* The closed station on this line that was in Cumbria was Alston.

** Originally named Featherstone until 1 January 1902.

*** Originally named Shaft Hill until closure in May 1853. Reopened as Shafthill in December 1862 and renamed Coanwood on 1 March 1885.

Featherstone Park Station.

On 26 August 1846 the Newcastle & Carlisle Railway was authorised by an Act of Parliament to build a branch line up the South Tyne Valley from Haltwhistle via Alston to Nenthead, the latter two places being centres of lead mining. However, the company had second thoughts about this and the following year a second Act was obtained that allowed them to abandon the four miles of line beyond Alston and to take a slightly different route from Haltwhistle. The resulting thirteen-mile branch was single line and was opened in sections; the one from the junction at Haltwhistle to Shafthill opened for goods traffic in March 1851 and for passengers on 19 July, whilst the southern section from Alston northwards to Lambley opened for goods on 5 January 1852 and throughout to Haltwhistle on 17 November when Lambley Viaduct was completed. In the intervening months passengers had to walk over the viaduct's scaffolding to join connecting trains on either side. The railway company had purchased sufficient land to build a double-track line throughout with the exception of the Lambley Viaduct but this was never used; although all the other viaducts on the line were built wide enough for two tracks the branch remained single track throughout to the end of its life although its stations had passing loops.

Lambley Station.

Alston is the highest market town in England and sometimes suffers from winter snowfalls that used to cut it off by road for days on end. This was the reason for the passenger service on the line surviving until 1976 although it had been earmarked for closure in 1965 under the Beeching axe. The engine shed at Alston had already been closed in 1959 when steam-hauled passenger trains were replaced by modern diesel multiple unit (DMU) trains in an attempt to increase passenger numbers, but this was in vain. When Lambley Colliery closed in 1955, goods services were withdrawn from Coanwood and intermediate stations became unstaffed halts. Goods facilities were withdrawn from intermediate stations on various dates between 1960 and 1965 and in October 1966 'one engine in steam' working was introduced and the signal boxes were closed. The passenger service lingered on for another ten years until at last an all-weather road was built to Alston and the last train ran on 1 May 1976, the line closing completely two days later.

The passenger service in 1925 consisted of four trains in each direction, most of them taking 35 minutes. As there was no engine shed at Haltwhistle the service was worked from a small single-road engine shed adjoining the station at Alston, usually by a Class G5 0-4-4T or an 0-6-2T. In the days of 'one engine in steam' a Class J21 0-6-0 worked both the passenger and goods services on the branch. Latterly classes J39 0-6-0s and BR Standard 2-6-0s were used, followed by DMUs. In 1961 the DMU-worked service was six trains each way on weekdays and no less than eight on Saturdays but the usual journey time remained 35 minutes.

The line left from the east side of Haltwhistle Station and immediately curved south, climbing on a 1 in 80 gradient to cross the River South Tyne on the Alston Arches viaduct. A few miles further on, after crossing the Lambley viaduct with its nine 58-foot span arches and eight 28-foot spans at 110 feet above the River South Tyne, the line entered Lambley itself. This was a stone-built station standing on a sharp curve immediately beyond the viaduct. Its platform buildings were on the west side of the line with a signal box at the Haltwhistle end where a line ran off to Lambley colliery, from where Lord Carlisle's private railways continued on to Brampton. There wasn't enough room for a crossing loop at the station and passing goods trains had to be shunted into the colliery branch. The last station on the line in Northumberland was Slaggyford, beyond which the line climbed on a gradient of 1 in 56 for a mile and crossed a number of viaducts before passing into what is now Cumbria and reaching Alston Station, having climbed 540 feet from Haltwhistle.

Broomhill Station.

Amble Branch

Passenger service withdrawn	7 July 1930
Distance	5 ³/₄ miles
Company	York, Newcastle & Berwick Railway

Stations closed	*Date of closure*
Chevington (East Coast Main Line)	15 September 1958
Broomhill	7 July 1930
Amble	7 July 1930

On 5 September 1849 the York, Newcastle & Berwick Railway opened a freight-only line from a junction on their main line near Chevington to the port of Amble. This town lies at the mouth of the River Coquet and prospered as a port in the nineteenth century as collieries were opened in the area. The branch was built primarily to carry coal from the collieries to the staithes in the harbour and Amble's heyday was probably in the 1920s when it handled some 750,000 tons of coal per year.

The line was single track from Chevington to Broomhill and double track from Broomhill to Amble. In 1878 an intermediate station was opened at Broomhill with a single platform on the down side of the line and the following year a new station at Amble was opened and a passenger service from Chevington commenced. At Chevington the Amble passenger trains left from the down side bay platform and ran parallel to the main line for about one and a quarter miles to Amble Junction where a gantry signal box straddled the main line. The branch line was almost level with only a few shallow cuttings or low embankments. Amble's station had a single passenger platform on the down side and the line continued for some 500 yards beyond it onto coal staithes. The station building was a two-storey brick structure with the first floor at platform level and the goods yard and shed stood to the southwest of the platform.

The branch was worked by an engine from Alnmouth Shed, usually a Class D22 4-4-0 or an F8 2-4-2T on a one-coach train and the service normally gave connections with main-line trains at Chevington, although some trains ran through between Amble and Morpeth. Passenger business was good until the advent of buses in the area after the First World War; in 1923 the service was only seven weekday trains in each direction and the line didn't survive the Great Depression, passenger services being withdrawn on 7 July 1930. General goods services survived until 1964 but 6 October 1969 saw the last coal train and complete closure of the line. Both Broomhill and Amble stations have been demolished, all the Northumberland collieries are now gone, and today the town of Amble is best known for tourism.

The Blyth & Tyne Railway

The Blyth & Tyne Railway operated a network of lines built primarily for carrying coal to the coast and to the north bank of the Tyne; the carriage of passengers was very much a secondary consideration. Blyth's long-time importance as a port for the output of the Northumberland collieries can be gauged from the fact that in 1961 it shipped out nearly 6,900,000 tons of coal, more than any other port in Britain. Some parts of the Blyth & Tyne Railway, which was taken over by the North Eastern Railway in August 1874, are now completely closed, some are parts of the Tyneside Metro system and others are only open for freight services. This section from pages 16 to 21 deals with the parts that have lost their timetabled passenger services and have not been incorporated into the Metro, while giving a history of the railway as a whole.

Percy Main — Blyth

Passenger service withdrawn	22 September 1964	*Stations closed*	*Date of closure*
Distance	11 ½ miles	Hartley	2 November 1964
		Newsham	2 November 1964
Stations closed	*Date of closure*	Blyth	2 November 1964
Percy Main *	11 August 1980		
Prospect Hill	27 June 1964	* Reopened on the Metro line on 14 November 1982.
Backworth **	27 June 1964	** Originally named Holywell until April 1860.
Seghill	2 November 1964	*** Originally named Seaton Delaval Colliery until August 1864.
Seaton Delaval ***	2 November 1964	

Seaton Delaval Station, 25 June 1950.

Blyth Station.

The Seghill Railway opened its line from Percy Main to Seghill for coal traffic on 1 June 1840 and for passenger traffic on 28 August in the following year. In 1846 it extended its line to Hartley and then, on 3 March 1847 and now called the Blyth, Seghill & Percy Main Railway, it finally reached Newsham and Blyth. On 3 August 1850 it extended its passenger services north from Newsham to Bedlington over the privately owned Bedlington Coal Company's line and on 1 January 1853 it became a constituent of the newly formed Blyth & Tyne Railway Company. This company then went on in 1855 to purchase outright the line from Newsham to Bedlington and on 1 April 1858 to extend the line to its own station at Morpeth. This was built alongside the North Eastern Railway's station and was shared with the Wansbeck Railway but following the rebuilding of the North Eastern's station in 1880 the Blyth & Tyne's passenger station was closed and was converted into two cottages, its passenger trains using a bay platform at the new station.

Newsham Station.

Newsham — Morpeth

Passenger service withdrawn	22 September 1964	*Stations closed*		*Date of closure*
Distance	8 miles	Choppington		3 April 1950
		Hepscot		3 April 1950
Stations closed	*Date of closure*	Morpeth (Blyth & Tyne station)		24 May 1880
Bebside *	2 November 1964			
Bedlington	2 November 1964	* Originally named Cowpen Lane until April 1860.		

Bedlington Station, 1963.

Newbiggin-by-the-Sea Branch

Passenger service withdrawn	22 September 1964	*Stations closed*	*Date of closure*
Distance	5 1/2 miles	Ashington *	2 November 1964
		Newbiggin-by-the-Sea	2 November 1964
Stations closed	*Date of closure*		
North Seaton	2 November 1964	* Originally named Hirst until 1 October 1889.	

Further expansion followed with a branch from Bedlington to North Seaton being opened on 7 November 1859; this was extended to Newbiggin-on-Sea on 1 March 1872. The Act of Parliament for this line empowered it to run all the way from Bedlington to Warkworth with Newbiggin being served by a branch from a junction at Ashington; however, what was intended to be the main line straight ahead from Ashington to Warkworth was never built, which is why the line took such a sharp turn to the east from Ashington to head for Newbiggin along what had been intended as a branch.

In 1923 there were 21 weekday passenger trains in either direction between Bedlington and Newbiggin whilst the Blyth branch saw no fewer than 39 daily and eight Sunday passenger trains to Blyth and 41 in the opposite direction, the majority of them being either branch line trains to and from Newsham or trains to and from Monkseaton. There were also eight weekday and three Sunday trains that ran between Manors North and Morpeth via Backworth.

Avenue Branch

		Stations closed	Date of closure
Passenger service withdrawn	3 July 1882	*Stations closed*	*Date of closure*
Distance	4 miles	Cullercoats (Blyth & Tyne station)	3 July 1882
		Tynemouth (Blyth & Tyne station)	3 July 1882

Stations closed	Date of closure
	Date of closure
The Avenue	27 June 1864
Whitley (Blyth & Tyne station) *	3 July 1882

* Renamed as Monkseaton on 3 July 1882, rather than closed outright.
Closed and replaced by the second Monkseaton Station on 25 July 1915.

The signal box at North Seaton Station on the Newbiggin-by-the-Sea branch.

On the southern section of the Blyth & Tyne Railway the line that ran from Hartley to Tynemouth (the Avenue branch) was opened in October 1860 but was superseded in 1882 by a newer line built by the North Eastern Railway, which had taken over the Blyth & Tyne Railway in 1874. The new line ran nearer the coast and now forms part of the Tyneside Metro. On the Blyth & Tyne's main line a junction was made south of Holywell in 1864 to join the newly opened 'City Branch' from Newcastle to Monkseaton and the line south of this junction through Prospect Hill to Percy Main was closed to passenger services on 27 June 1864.

The Blyth & Tyne's station in Newcastle, opened in 1864, was at New Bridge Street but this closed in 1909 when the line was diverted to a new station at Manors North and many of its services started or terminated here. In 1943 its trains to Morpeth were diverted beyond Bedlington to run to Newbiggin, which left the section from Bedlington to Morpeth with only two trains per day, worked by Sentinel steam railcars. Between Manors North and Backworth the Newbiggin trains shared the tracks with the electric services to Tynemouth.

There were two major timber viaducts on the northern section of the Blyth & Tyne's lines. One was between Bebside and Bedlington where the River Blyth was crossed on a structure 80 feet high and 770 feet in length that was erected in 1850; in 1929 it was replaced by a more conventional design. The other viaduct was over the River Wansbeck near North Seaton; it was built in 1859 and consisted of 43 25-feet spans with a maximum height of 86 feet. It was replaced in 1927 by a new 14-span plate girder bridge.

Passenger services in the area in LNER days were operated by classes F8 2-4-2T and G5 0-4-4T engines, followed by Gresley's V1 and V3 2-6-2T classes but a number of Sentinel steam railcars also worked in the area, mainly between Morpeth, Blyth and Monkseaton. Nowadays most of the Blyth & Tyne's main line is still well used by freight trains serving industries on or near the coast and it is also used very occasionally by diverted passenger services and by railtours. A few faint traces remain of the junctions at Backworth and Hartley and the station platforms are still extant at Bedlington and Ashington. The line is in good condition throughout; it has been reduced to single track between Benton North Junction (its present-day access from the south) and Newsham South Junction but elsewhere it remains double track.

Border Counties Railway *

Passenger service withdrawn	15 October 1956	*Stations closed*	*Date of closure*
Distance	42 miles	Tarset	15 October 1956
Company	Border Counties Railway	Thorneyburn	15 October 1956
		Falstone	15 October 1956
Stations closed	*Date of closure*	Plashetts	15 October 1956
Wall	19 September 1955	Lewiefield Halt	15 October 1956
Humshaugh **	15 October 1956	Kielder Forest ***	15 October 1956
Chollerton	15 October 1956	Deadwater	15 October 1956
Barrasford	15 October 1956		
Wark	15 October 1956		
Countess Park	1 February 1861		
Reedsmouth	15 October 1956		
Bellingham	15 October 1956		
Charlton	1 October 1862		

* Closed stations on this line that were in Scotland were Saughtree and Riccarton Junction.
** Originally named Chollerford until 1 August 1919.
*** Originally named Kielder until 1 October 1948.

Barrasford Station.

This was a 42-mile single-track line running from Hexham on the Newcastle & Carlisle Railway to Riccarton on the Border Union Railway. In 1854 the Border Counties Railway (North Tyne Section) Act authorised the building of a 26-mile line from Border Counties Junction about a mile west of Hexham to Belling Burn near Falstone, with Robert Nicholson appointed as its engineer. However, before the work could commence, Robert Nicholson died and his nephew J.F. Tone took over as engineer for the line. The contract for the first section of line was awarded to William Hutchinson who subsequently went on to build the entire line. On 11 December 1855 the first sod was cut at a ceremony at Tyne Green west of Hexham and almost immediately the company's directors ordered a survey to be made for a route into Scotland; however, when this was presented to Parliament as a Bill it was rejected. In the meantime the line opened as far as Chollerford on 5 April 1858. The directors were more successful with their Bill in the following year and on 1 August 1859 the Border Counties Railway (Liddesdale & Deviations) Act authorised the extension of the line to Riccarton on the Border Union Railway, which was owned by the North British Railway.

Tarset Station.

In 1860 the North British and Border Counties Railway Amalgamation Act was passed; this gave the North British Railway a through line from Edinburgh to Hexham and in 1862 it achieved its great ambition of reaching Newcastle-upon-Tyne by obtaining running powers for its trains over North Eastern Railway metals. But this ambition was achieved at a high price: in exchange for granting the North British running powers from Hexham to Newcastle the North Eastern were granted running powers over the North British's main line from Berwick to Edinburgh and subsequently ran Anglo-Scottish east coast main line expresses themselves throughout between Newcastle and Edinburgh. It was a bad bargain for the North British; their line ran through moorland and farmland but it was a sparsely populated area and there was very little industry apart from a colliery at Plashetts. They had exchanged operations on a profitable main line for those on an unrenumerative branch line.

The line opened to Falstone on 2 September 1861 and was completed throughout on 2 May 1862 but, although Board of Trade approval had been received, the first goods train didn't run until 24 June and passengers had to wait until 1 July because of delays on the Border Union Railway. Although the line was always single track throughout, it was built to allow for double track except for the Hexham viaduct and its course northwards followed the North Tyne for almost its entire route with a ruling gradient of 1 in 100. From Border Counties Junction at Hexham it ran northwards to Reedsmouth where it was joined by the line from Morpeth trailing in from the east. It then turned north-westwards and followed the river valley to Kielder, then climbed to the source of the river at Deadwater which was the line's last station in England. At the line's terminus at Riccarton Junction the station's sole purpose was to provide interchange facilities for passengers changing from Edinburgh – Carlisle trains into Reedsmouth, Hexham and Newcastle trains; the station had no road access and the community living adjacent to the station comprised only railway employees and their families.

Plashetts Station.

The service between Riccarton Junction and Newcastle was worked throughout by North British Railway and subsequently London & North Eastern Railway 4-4-0 and 2-6-0 locomotives of classes D20, D31, D32, D49 and K1 shedded at Blaydon. In the 1930s North British 'Scott' Class engines shedded at Hawick also worked this service. For many years the Border Counties line service consisted of three trains in each direction daily but with the increase in population in the Kielder area due to the afforestation programme a midday train to Hexham was introduced on Saturdays with a 2225 return.

A showman's traction engine, names 'The Busy Bee', with Bellingham Station building behind.

Leaving the Newcastle & Carlisle line at Border Counties Junction immediately west of Hexham station the line immediately crossed the Tyne on a long low skewed four-span viaduct of which only the piers remain today. Reedsmouth was the junction with the Wansbeck line which trailed in from the right and necessitated the junction station being rebuilt 100 yards to the south. An amusing anomaly here is that the village is actually called Redesmouth but the railway authorities insisted on calling the station Reedsmouth! Beyond Falstone the line is nowadays submerged beneath Kielder Water for several miles, covering the former station at Plashetts. Beyond that was Lewiefield Halt which was opened in 1935 for the arrival of those to be discharged into a Ministry of Labour training camp for long-term unemployed miners and shipyard workers (it was later a home for conscientious objectors during the Second World War and finally for displaced people from Eastern Europe).

The passenger service was withdrawn over the whole length of the line on 15 October 1956, following damage to a bridge near Hexham, and to goods traffic on 1 September 1958, except for Bellingham to Reedsmouth which connected to the Wansbeck line. However, even this was closed in November 1963 and rural Northumberland has remained silent ever since. Many of the former stations have been converted into substantial private houses.

Newcastle — Blaydon via Scotswood

Passenger service withdrawn	4 October 1982	*Stations closed*	*Date of closure*
Distance	3 miles	Elswick	2 January 1967
Company	Newcastle & Carlisle Railway	Scotswood Works Halt *	27 September 1924
		Scotswood (Blaydon line platforms)	1 May 1967

Stations closed	*Date of closure*
Newcastle Shot Tower	1 March 1847
Newcastle Forth Bank	1 January 1851

* Temporarily opened between 1940 and 1944.

The Newcastle & Carlisle Railway's first station in Newcastle opened on 21 May 1839 in Railway Street close to the shot tower, from which it took its name. However, a bigger and better station was opened at Forth Bank on 1 March 1847 and the earlier station was closed. This new station in turn lasted until the end of 1851 when the Newcastle & Carlisle trains began running into the newly opened Central Station, whereupon the Forth Bank station was converted into one of the largest goods depots in Europe.

This line was the Newcastle & Carlisle's route westwards out of the city and ran through a thoroughly industrial area along the north bank of the Tyne with the extensive buildings of Vickers-Armstrong's Elswick engineering works on the left and row after row of terraced houses opposite the works on the steep hillside to the right of the line. The only notable engineering feature was the viaduct across the Tyne from Scotswood to Blaydon which was originally built of timber in 1839 but, having been damaged by fire in 1860, was replaced by a temporary single-track bridge

The former Newcastle Shot Tower Station, *c.*1910. By that time the station had been closed for around 63 years.

in 1861 and by yet another in 1865. Eventually a new double-track six-span hogback girder bridge with wrought-iron girders resting on five cast-iron piers was built in 1871. The bridge was designed by T.E. Harrison and built by Palmer's of Jarrow at a cost of £20,000. It was strengthened in 1943 but when expensive repairs were again necessary in 1982 it was decided to close this section of the line and re-route trains over the King Edward Bridge and along the hitherto freight-only line of 1907 via Dunston to rejoin the route near Blaydon. Tracks were removed west of Elswick, leaving only a one-mile siding from Newcastle, and the Scotswood Viaduct now carries only water and gas mains across the river.

Elswick Station.

Elswick Station, which opened on 2 September 1889, was situated at the western end of the Elswick Works and had a 25-feet wide island platform and a long glazed awning which survived until June 1962. Like most urban lines, it suffered from road competition in the twentieth century; the works traffic kept it in business for many years but on 11 September 1961 Elswick was demoted to an unstaffed halt. It was closed completely in 1967 and the platform quickly demolished. Scotswood Works Halt, which was opened in 1915 for wartime workers at Armstrong Whitworth's munitions factory, had an even shorter life. It was closed in 1924, reopened in 1940, closed again in 1944 and was finally demolished 1948. The halt was situated about 700 yards east of Scotswood Station and was a 150-yard-long island platform that was built at Armstrong Whitworth's expense. An additional platform was added in 1919, this time built at the Ministry of Munitions' expense. The halt was never advertised in the public timetable but it was well used, principally by workmen's trains.

The first station at Scotswood opened on 21 October 1839 and was extended on 12 July 1875 when the North Wylam branch was built. The station had four platforms, the two northerly ones for the North Wylam line and the two southerly ones for the Newcastle & Carlisle line across the river to Blaydon. These station buildings burned down on 17 October 1879 and were not rebuilt until the mid-1880s when the new station building at the east end of the Blaydon-bound platform was constructed in brick and the two sets of platforms were connected by both an overbridge and a subway. The station was busy until the 1930s when buses began to drain away much of its traffic and in its later years the train service calling here was at irregular intervals and infrequent. After closure in 1966 the station platforms and buildings were demolished by 1972.

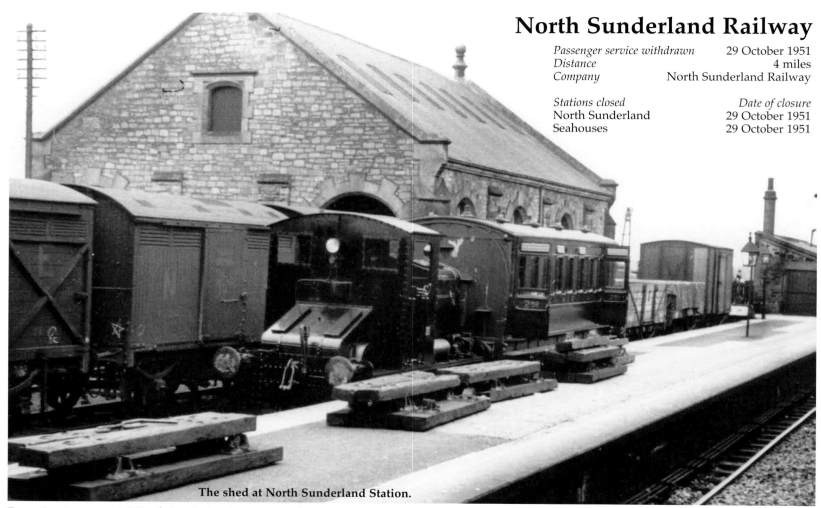

North Sunderland Railway

Passenger service withdrawn	29 October 1951
Distance	4 miles
Company	North Sunderland Railway

Stations closed	Date of closure
North Sunderland	29 October 1951
Seahouses	29 October 1951

The shed at North Sunderland Station.

From time immemorial North Sunderland, situated eight miles southeast of Belford, has been a fishing port. In 1889 its facilities were expanded so much that its harbour was able to accommodate up to 300 fishing vessels and the port became known as Seahouses to avoid confusion with Sunderland in County Durham. Because of the poor state of the roads between the harbour and the nearest railhead at Chathill, local merchants and fishermen petitioned the North Eastern Railway for a branch line; when their request was rejected they decided to form their own company.

Seahouses Station.

The North Sunderland Railway Act of 1892 authorised construction of a single-line branch from Chathill to Seahouses with intermediate stations at Fleetham and North Sunderland. Construction began in 1896 and at an early stage the planned station at Fleetham was abandoned to cut costs. The line was almost level with a few small earthworks, shallow cuttings and low embankments. In 1898 the company was authorised under the Light Railway Act of 1896 to extend the line from Seahouses to Bamburgh (this was never built) and to operate the line as a light railway. It opened to goods traffic on 1 August 1898 and to passengers on 18 December that year. The two stations at North Sunderland and Seahouses were quite rudimentary and both were constructed of corrugated iron; even the engine shed and goods shed were of the same material.

The company only ever owned two locomotives, Bamburgh, which was an 0-6-0 saddle tank of 1898, and The Lady Armstrong, which was a diesel electric of 1934. Both were scrapped in 1949 although by that date they had been in store for some time and needed repairs. Other locomotives were hired in as and when required; these included classes Y1 and Y3 Sentinel locomotives, Y7 0-4-0T, J71 and J79 0-6-0Ts and an ex-LYR 0-4-0ST. A Class Y7 0-4-0T was working the branch at the time of its closure in October 1951 but taxis had also to be used when there was no engine available. The passenger coaches were a motley collection that had been bought over the years second hand from the Highland, North Eastern and Great Eastern railways. The train service was usually five or six trains daily in each direction with a summer Sunday service from 1935 to 1939. The journey time was initially fifteen minutes but in later years this was increased to 20 minutes.

Goods facilities were withdrawn in February 1928. By 1939 the company was in a serious financial position and the London & North Eastern Railway took over its management. When the railways were nationalised in 1948 the line was inherited by the newly formed North Eastern Region of British Railways who, in 1951, ended the arrangement by which the company borrowed locomotives.

The last train ran on 27 October 1951 and the line was closed completely two days later. It was then discovered that because of an oversight the North Sunderland Light Railway Company Limited of 1898 had never been legally registered; this was belatedly done on 25 April 1952 and the company was formally wound up 53 days later. In 1953 the track was lifted by the Motherwell Machinery and Scrap Company and the buildings were demolished. The site of Seahouses Station is now the main car park for the village.

North Wylam Loop

Passenger service withdrawn	11 March 1968	*Stations closed*	*Date of closure*
Distance	6 ½ miles	Newburn	15 September 1958
Company	Scotswood, Newburn & Wylam Railway & Dock Company	Heddon-on-the-Wall	15 September 1958
		North Wylam	11 March 1968

Stations closed   *Date of closure*

Scotswood (North Wylam line platforms) *   1 May 1967   * No service from 3 September 1966.

Lemington   15 September 1958

The Scotswood, Newburn & Wylam Railway & Dock Company (SN&WR&DC) Act was passed by Act of Parliament on 16 June 1871 and construction began the following April. On 12 July 1875 the company opened a loop line on the Newcastle & Carlisle Railway from a junction at Scotswood Station to West Wylam Junction near Prudhoe, running through a number of small towns along the north bank of the Tyne. However, the dock was never built because the Tyne proved to be too shallow and was not dredged as far up river as Scotswood; thus, on 7 April 1876 a further Act of Parliament was passed that allowed the company to abandon the proposed dock.

North Wylam Loop   33

From the outset the line was operated by the North Eastern Railway on behalf of the SN&WR&DC who it absorbed on 29 June 1883. The line followed most of the route of the Wylam Waggonway between Scotswood and North Wylam; it was opened from Newburn to West Wylam on 13 May 1876 and onward to West Wylam Junction on the south bank of the Tyne in October of that year after completion of the bridge across the river. In spite of being a loop line with facilities for running through to Prudhoe and beyond, passenger services from Newcastle generally terminated at North Wylam. These trains used the two northern platforms at Scotswood that were opened on 12 July 1875 and had wooden buildings. On the way to the final station at North Wylam the line passed George Stephenson's birthplace at Street Cottage, which stands at the lineside. Beyond the station the line crossed the Tyne to join the Newcastle & Carlisle main line at Prudhoe via Hagg Bank Bridge, a single-span wrought-iron viaduct that was restored for pedestrians and cyclists in 1997.

Locomotive No. 7658 at North Wylam Station.

In 1923 there were ten weekday trains in each direction, in later years these were reduced to eight. The passenger service survived until 1968 but in 1972 the line was cut back from North Wylam Junction to Newburn and the track was lifted; on 1 December 1986 the remaining section to Scotswood was also closed. The former trackbed is now largely the North Tyne Cycleway and footpath, which is part of the Tyne Riverside Country Park.

North Wylam Loop

Ponteland & Darras Hall Branch

Passenger service withdrawn	17 June 1929	*Stations closed*	*Date of closure*
Distance	8 ½ miles	Ponteland	17 June 1929
Company	Gosforth & Ponteland Light Railway	Darras Hall	17 June 1929

Stations closed	*Date of closure*
South Gosforth *	17 June 1929
West Gosforth **	17 June 1929
Coxlodge ***	17 June 1929
Kenton Bank ****	17 June 1929
Callerton	17 June 1929

* Originally named Gosforth until 1 March 1905. Reopened on Metro on 10 May 1981.

** Reopened as Regent Centre on Metro on 10 May 1981.

*** Reopened as Fawdon on Metro on 10 May 1981.

**** Originally named Kenton until 1 July 1923. Reopened as Bank Foot on Metro on 10 May 1981.

Two electric locomotives on display at South Gosforth Station, for the benefit of a rail tour, 29 September 1963.

Under the terms of the Light Railways Act of 1896 the Gosforth & Ponteland Light Railway Bill was submitted to Parliament by the North Eastern Railway on 29 November 1898. In 1899 the Bill received Royal Assent for the building of the Ponteland Light Railway from South Gosforth, then known as Gosforth. The six and three-quarter mile route, which branched off the Newcastle to Whitley Bay route at South Gosforth, ran on single track with gradients in both directions as steep as 1 in 55. There were several level crossings over public roads but major roads and mineral lines were crossed by bridges.

Construction began in 1900 but it wasn't until 1 March 1905 that goods services commenced, followed by passenger services on 1 June. Initially, there were plans to electrify the line as an extension of Newcastle's 'Coast Circle' line but these were abandoned when passenger numbers failed to reach expectations. However, a high-class residential development was built at Darras Hall in 1907 when a group of Newcastle businessmen bought land southwest of Ponteland with the aim of creating a 'garden city' for professional and managerial residents. In November 1908 the Little Callerton Railway Bill for a one and a quarter mile extension of line to Darras Hall was submitted to Parliament; the requisite approval was obtained the following year but it wasn't until 27 September 1913 that the Darras extension was opened to passengers and to goods on 1 October that year. Its single track was built largely on an embankment but with space for a second track should traffic warrant it, but this extension was a financial failure. The estate grew slowly and its loose grid of roads with detached houses at a maximum density of six per acre limited the number of potential passengers.

Kenton Station, *c*.1904.

Although the 1903 North Eastern Railway electrification scheme originally included the railway the line was steam operated from its opening in June 1905 until it closed to passengers in June 1929. Passenger services between South Gosforth and Ponteland/Darras Hall were normally operated by push-and-pull units of two carriages attached to a Class G4 0-4-4 locomotive that was based at Heaton Shed. There were nine or ten weekday services to Ponteland but only four on Sundays; the journey time being ten minutes. The Sunday trains were withdrawn by June 1920 and the scanty provision of three weekday trains plus the need to change at South Gosforth was an additional disincentive to use the service. No industrial development was permitted at Darras Hall except for the North Eastern Railway's goods yard, so even goods traffic was restricted.

In the mid-1920s Sentinel steam railcars took over the Ponteland Branch services, running through to Newcastle Central. Goods trains were operated by LNER Class J24, J25, J27 and J39 0-6-0 and Q6 0-8-0 locomotives and latterly by BR Class 25 and Class 40 diesels. Class V1 and V3 2-6-2 locomotives occasionally appeared with enthusiasts' specials and when Royal Trains were stabled overnight on the line.

Newcastle Corporation buses which served Darras Hall and provided direct routes between Kenton, Gosforth and Newcastle took the traffic from the trains and on 17 June 1929 passenger services were withdrawn from South Gosforth onwards, parcels traffic ending on 5 January 1935. In the 1960s redundant Coast Circular electric stock was stored at Ponteland and Callerton. On 2 August 1954 goods services were withdrawn from the Darras Hall extension, from Ponteland in 1967, and all freight workings ended totally on the branch on 6 March 1989. However, this was not quite the end of the branch because in 1981 the Newcastle Metro had opened from South Gosforth to Bank Foot (formerly Kenton Bank) and on 17 November 1991 it was extended from there to Newcastle Airport, involving a very short branch from the Ponteland route after Callerton.

Riverside Branch

Passenger service withdrawn	23 July 1973
Distance	6 ½ miles
Company	Newcastle & North Shields Railway

Stations closed	*Date of closure*
Byker	5 April 1954
St Peters	23 July 1973
St Anthonys	12 September 1960
Walker *	23 July 1973
Carville	23 July 1973
Point Pleasant	23 July 1973
Willington Quay	23 July 1973

* Originally named Low Walker until 13 May 1889.

On 20 June 1839 the Newcastle & North Shields Railway opened a line from Newcastle to North Shields and later to Tynemouth. On 13 July 1871 its successor, the North Eastern Railway, was authorised to build a branch from it to serve the rapidly growing industrial area on the north bank of the Tyne. This new line, known as the Riverside Branch, was a double-track loop which left the Tynemouth line at Riverside Junction, between Manors and Heaton, and rejoined it at Percy Main West Junction which was situated to the west of Percy Main Station. The line necessitated quite heavy earthworks and severe curvature, and the gradients were fairly heavy.

The loop line opened on 1 May 1879 but by the early years of the twentieth century it was suffering severe competition from a frequent tram service in the area. In an attempt to counter this threat it was one of the Tyneside lines that were electrified, with services commencing on 1st July 1904; the electric trains were supplanted by DMUs in 1967. However, when the Tyneside lines were converted to the Metro system in the 1970s this line was excluded. The smaller stations had already been closed and the passenger service was withdrawn from the remaining stations on 23 July 1973. The line was closed in sections between 31 May 1978 and 31 March 1988; part of the trackbed has now been converted into a cycleway and footpath known as Hadrian's Way which forms part of the C2C cycle route and the Hadrian's Wall National Trail.

The frequency of train services varied over the years, being linked to the area's prosperity or otherwise. In 1923 there were ten weekday services which ran from Newcastle Central through to Tynemouth over this route but by the 1960s only a limited peak service for the shipyards remained and the branch was recommended for closure under the 'Beeching Axe'. However, it was reprieved in 1964 and survived for several years more until road improvements had been completed in 1973. All the stations were subsequently demolished, apart from Carville where the station house has been turned into the Segedunum Business Centre.

The view from Rothbury signal box, Novbember 1963.

Rothbury Branch

Passenger service withdrawn	15 September 1952
Distance	13 miles
Company	Northumberland Central Railway

Stations closed	*Date of closure*
Longwitton	15 September 1952
Ewesley	15 September 1952
Fontburn Halt	15 September 1952
Brinkburn	15 September 1952
Rothbury	15 September 1952

The Northumberland Central Railway Act of 1863 authorised the building of a line from a junction with the Wansbeck Railway, near Hartburn, to Ford, with a branch to Cornhill on the Berwick & Kelso Railway. However, the line was never continued beyond Rothbury and a further Act in 1867 authorised abandonment of the line beyond that town. In consequence the railway finished up as a thirteen-mile single-track branch from Scotsgap to Rothbury that opened for passengers and goods on 19 October 1870. In July 1872 the Northumberland Central Railway amalgamated with the North British Railway.

The branch left the Wansbeck Railway at Scotsgap Junction after running in parallel for about half a mile beyond the station. Beyond Ewesley the line curved right and crossed the River Font on a stone viaduct consisting of twelve 30-foot arches. Rothbury Station was upgraded in 1899 with fairly substantial station buildings and there were also refuge sidings, a goods shed and a loading bank because a considerable amount of livestock was handled for local farmers. Race specials to Rothbury races were popular and in the 1930s circular excursions, often using dining cars, were run from Newcastle to Rothbury via Morpeth; after a stop for lunch the return was via Scotsgap, Reedsmouth and Hexham.

By the winter of 1938/39 there were three trains in each direction between Rothbury and Morpeth and a late evening return trip on Saturdays, all worked by Rothbury Shed. Engines shedded at Rothbury were, at various times, classes F8 2-4-2T, G5 0-4-4T and J21 0-6-0. The passenger service on the line was withdrawn on 15 September 1952, the same day as the Wansbeck Railway and for the same reasons. The line was closed completely on 9 November 1963 and the track was lifted by mid 1964.

An old crane in the goods yard at Rothbury Station, November 1963.

Tweedmouth — Kelso Branch *

Passenger service withdrawn	15 June 1964
Distance	22 ¹/₄ miles
Company	Newcastle & Berwick Railway

Stations closed	*Date of closure*
Tweedmouth (East Coast Main Line)	15 June 1964
Velvet Hall	4 July 1955
Norham	15 June 1964
Twizell	4 July 1955

Stations closed	*Date of closure*
Coldstream **	15 June 1964
Sunilaws ***	4 July 1955

* The closed stations on this line that were in Scotland were Carham, Sprouston and Kelso.
** Originally named Cornhill until 1 October 1873.
*** Originally named Wark until 1 October 1874.

Tweedmouth Station, 14 April 1963.

Velvet Hall Station, *c.*1910.

The Newcastle & Berwick Railway Act of 31 July 1845 included powers to build a double-track branch line from Tweedmouth to Kelso. By 27 July 1849 the line had opened to Sprouston and, on 1 June 1851, it opened throughout to Kelso, making an end-on junction with the North British Railway's branch from St Boswells. The double-track line ran through a narrow belt of rich farming land between the Tweed and the Cheviot Hills and its gradients were fairly easy although with a few difficult curves. A station had already been opened on 29 March 1847 on the main line at Tweedmouth, which is on the opposite bank of the River Tweed from Berwick. This now became the junction for the Kelso Branch and an engine shed was built here to service the line. To show the area's importance an impressive hotel, now demolished, was built on the west front of the station with its entrance facing towards Berwick.

Through trains from Berwick to Kelso had to cross the Royal Border Bridge and reverse at Tweedmouth, leaving from the down platform and curving away to the west almost immediately at Tweedmouth Junction. About half a mile southwest of Twizell Station the River Till was crossed by the six-arch Twizell Viaduct which is 89 feet high and nearly 400 feet long. In 2005 this viaduct was renovated and now forms part of a public footpath. The next station was situated in the English village of Cornhill and bore that name until 1 October 1873 when it was renamed Coldstream although that town is actually across the River Tweed in Scotland! The junction for the branch to Alnwick was immediately beyond the station but the two lines ran side by side for about a mile before diverging. The next station towards Kelso was opened in July 1859 as Wark and was renamed Sunilaws on 1 August 1871. It was the last station on the line in Northumberland; beyond it was Carham where the village was in England but its station was in Scotland, then Sprouston where the North Eastern Railway's line made an end-on junction with the North British Railway's line one mile west of the station, and finally Kelso itself where the trains from Tweedmouth terminated and made connections with the North British Railway's branches to Jedburgh and to St Boswells on the Waverley route between Carlisle and Edinburgh.

Coldstream Station, 14 April 1963.

The line was never well used from the outset; its most likely purpose was to pre-empt the North British Railway from gaining access to the Tweed Valley. In 1923 there were five weekday trains from Berwick to Kelso and six in the opposite direction, two of these diverging at Coldstream and running through to and from Alnwick. There were also two Sunday trains. In 1953 there were four weekday trains in each direction, all running between Berwick and St Boswells but by 1961 these had been reduced to two.

The line had a brief period of glory in 1948 when, following the floods on 12 August when six bridges were washed away on the East Coast Main Line, Anglo-Scottish expresses were diverted via the Waverley route to St Boswells and then over the Kelso branch to Tweedmouth for the next three months. This led to a new long-distance non-stop record being created because the 'Elizabethan' train (a service that ran from 1953 to 1962) normally ran non-stop from Edinburgh Waverley to London Kings Cross, a distance of 393 miles. Because of the diversion caused by the floods, the express was booked to stop at Hardengreen for banking assistance up the steep gradient to Falahill on the Waverley route and also to stop at either Galashiels or Tweedmouth to refill the tender tank with water. On 7 September, Driver Jimmy Swan of Edinburgh's Haymarket Shed, having taken careful note on previous runs of his engine's hill-climbing capabilities and water consumption, omitted both stops and set a new British non-stop record of 408 $\frac{1}{2}$ miles. More flooding occurred in August 1954 and line was used again for a couple of days but withdrawal of passenger services began in the following year, leaving only Coldstream and Norham open for passengers. The line struggled on for a few years more but on 15 June 1964 passenger services were withdrawn from the remaining stations and the line closed completely on 29 March of the following year.

Tyne Commission Quay Branch

Passenger service withdrawn	4 May 1970
Distance	2 miles
Company	Northumberland Central Railway

Stations closed	*Date of closure*
Tyne Commission Quay	4 May 1970

This short branch line was opened on 15 June 1928, principally to allow boat trains from London Kings Cross to deliver their passengers onto the quayside adjacent to their connecting ship to Scandinavia and other places. These trains were worked from Newcastle along the former Blyth & Tyne line as far as Percy Main where there was once a small station on the curve joining the former North Eastern Railway and the Blyth & Tyne lines. After passing the site of this station, the trains reversed at Percy Main North, passed under the Newcastle to Tynemouth line, and eventually joined the Tyne Improvement Commission's lines to reach the quay. The outbreak of the Second World War led to the line being closed from 2 October 1939 until November 1945 when the service was resumed. Until 1968 the passenger carriages had been fitted with vacuum brakes but problems were experienced when new air-braked carriages were introduced. This led to the through service from London being discontinued from 1 January 1969 and the line was closed completely on 4 May 1970, buses being provided from Newcastle Central Station to connect with the boat services.

Wansbeck Railway

Passenger service withdrawn	15 September 1952	*Stations closed*	*Date of closure*
Distance	25 ¹/₄ miles	Angerton	15 September 1952
Company	Wansbeck Valley Railway Company	Middleton North	15 September 1952
		Scotsgap	15 September 1952
		Knowesgate	15 September 1952
Stations closed	*Date of closure*	Woodburn	15 September 1952
Morpeth (Blyth & Tyne station)	24 May 1880	Reedsmouth	15 October 1956 (see Border Counties Railway)
Meldon	15 September 1952		

Scotsgap Station.

The Wansbeck Railway Company Act of 1859 authorised the building of a line from Morpeth to Reedsmouth on the Border Counties Railway. A protégé of the North British Railway, this single-track line ran through an area of hill farming and was built with two things in mind: to serve the rural area the line ran through, and to connect the North British Railway's system at Reedsmouth to the Blyth & Tyne Railway at Morpeth. This route was thirteen miles longer than the North Eastern Railway's line from Edinburgh via Berwick but it would have given the North British Railway access to Newcastle via the Blyth & Tyne Railway, which was one of the few railways in the north east of England that was not yet controlled by the North Eastern Railway. The Wansbeck Valley Railway amalgamated with the North British Railway in 1863 and the latter's directors subsequently entered into discussions with the Blyth & Tyne Railway with a view to buying it outright. However, the North Eastern got wind of the negotiations and rapidly stepped in to buy the Blyth & Tyne themselves in 1874.

The North British Railway's original idea had been to run through trains from Edinburgh to Newcastle via Riccarton Junction, Reedsmouth and Morpeth but their plans changed after they had gained access to Newcastle in 1870 over the Border Counties Line via Hexham. They decided to operate a service from Morpeth to Rothbury via Scotsgap and to work Scotsgap to Reedsmouth as a separate section. On 23 July 1862 the line was opened to Scotsgap from the Blyth & Tyne's station at Morpeth which was built alongside the North Eastern Railway's station. It extended further west to Knowesgate in October the following year and opened fully to Reedsmouth on 1 May 1865.

Originally the line left the Blyth & Tyne station at Morpeth, passed over the Newcastle & Berwick Railway's line on a flyover and headed west, but in 1880 this was altered so that the line ran into the island platform at the latter's rebuilt station (by then the North Eastern Railway) and the flyover was removed. Scotsgap was the junction for the branch to Rothbury and was equipped with four sidings and a loading bank, warehouse and engine turntable. At one time troop trains used to run to Woodburn regularly in connection with the nearby military training centres at Otterburn and Redesdale. The line continued from here to its trailing junction with the Border Counties Railway at Reedsmouth.

The meagre passenger services ran from Reedsmouth to Scotsgap at 0753 and 1615 and connected at Scotsgap with the morning and evening trains from Rothbury to Morpeth; the same arrangement applied in the opposite direction. On Saturdays there was an additional train from Reedsmouth to connect with the midday train from Rothbury to Morpeth. The motive power for the services was usually a Class J21 0-6-0.

The passenger service on the whole length of the line was a pre-Beeching casualty, hard economic conditions resulting in its withdrawal on 15 September 1952. Goods services were withdrawn beyond Woodburn on 11 November 1963 and the last goods train of all ran on 29 September 1966. However, three days later the line's closure was marked by the 'Wansbeck Piper', an excursion organised by Gosforth Round Table in which Ivatt Class 4MT 2-6-0s Nos. 43000 and 43063 were coupled tender-to-tender with an eleven-coach train running Newcastle–Morpeth–Woodburn and return. The fare for this splendid excursion was 18/6d (92.5p). Next day the line closed forever.

Closed passenger stations on lines still open to passengers
Newcastle-upon-Tyne — Berwick-upon-Tweed (East Coast Main Line)

Stations closed	Date of closure	Stations closed	Date of closure
Heaton	11 August 1980	Christon Bank *	15 September 1958
Forest Hall	15 September 1958	Newham *	15 September 1958
Killingworth	15 September 1958	Lucker *	February 1953
Annitsford	15 September 1958	Belford	20 January 1968
Plessey	15 September 1958	Cragg Mill	September 1877
Stannington	15 September 1958	Smeafield	1 May 1930
Longhirst	29 October 1951	Beal	29 January 1968
Chevington	15 September 1958	Goswick	15 September 1958
Warkworth	15 September 1958	Scremerston *	8 July 1951
Lesbury	1851	Tweedmouth	15 June 1964
Longhoughton	18 June 1962		
Little Mill *	15 September 1958		

* Closed as a wartime economy measure between 5 May 1941 and 7 October 1946.

The exterior and interior of Christon Bank signal box.

Beal Station.

Newcastle-upon-Tyne — Carlisle

Gilsland Station.

Stations closed	Date of closure
Scotswood	3 September 1966
Ryton	5 July 1954
Fourstones	2 January 1967
Greenhead	2 January 1967
Gilsland	2 January 1967